Finding FOSSILS

by Susan Markowitz Meredith

Table of Contents

What Are Fossils?

Have you ever heard of dinosaurs? Dinosaurs are animals that lived millions of years ago.

How do we know about dinosaurs if they lived so long ago? That's right! We know about them because of fossils.

I'm Dr. Dee. I study fossils. Let's learn about fossils together.

Some fossils are parts of animals
or plants that lived long ago.

▼ These bones are parts of a dinosaur.

Other fossils are marks that were left by animals or plants that lived long ago.

▲ These footprints are marks left by a dinosaur.

How Are Fossils Made?

Most fossils are made when plant and animal parts or marks are saved in rock.

After an animal died, it was covered with sand and dirt. Over time, it was covered by more sand and dirt.

After a very long time, the sand and dirt turned into rock. Some parts of the animal were saved in the rock. The parts that were saved are fossils.

◀ The dinosaur dies. Its body falls to the ground.

◀ The body becomes covered in sand and dirt.

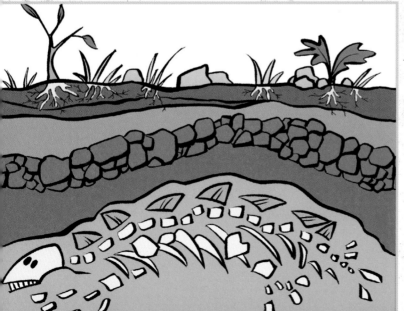

◀ The sand and dirt turn into rock around the bones.

Why Do People Study Fossils?

Fossils tell us what life was like millions of years ago. They help us learn about plants and animals that lived long ago.

▲ Scientists bring the fossils to a lab.
There they study the fossils.

◀ Fossils are found around the world. Most fossils
are found in rocky areas. Scientists use special tools
to dig them up.

People look at fossils to learn about dinosaurs. They put fossils together like pieces of a puzzle. They build models of dinosaurs.

Scientists use fossils to build dinosaur models. These models help them predict what dinosaurs looked like.

By looking at fossils, people think triceratops looked like this. ▶

What Are Some Different Kinds of Fossils?

You have just seen some dinosaur fossils. Now let's look at some other kinds of fossils.

▼ This is a fossil of a fish.

This is a fossil of a fern leaf.

This is a fossil, too! Insects are inside this yellow amber.

This amber was soft tree sap long ago. The insects got stuck in it. When the sap got hard and dry, the insects were saved inside.

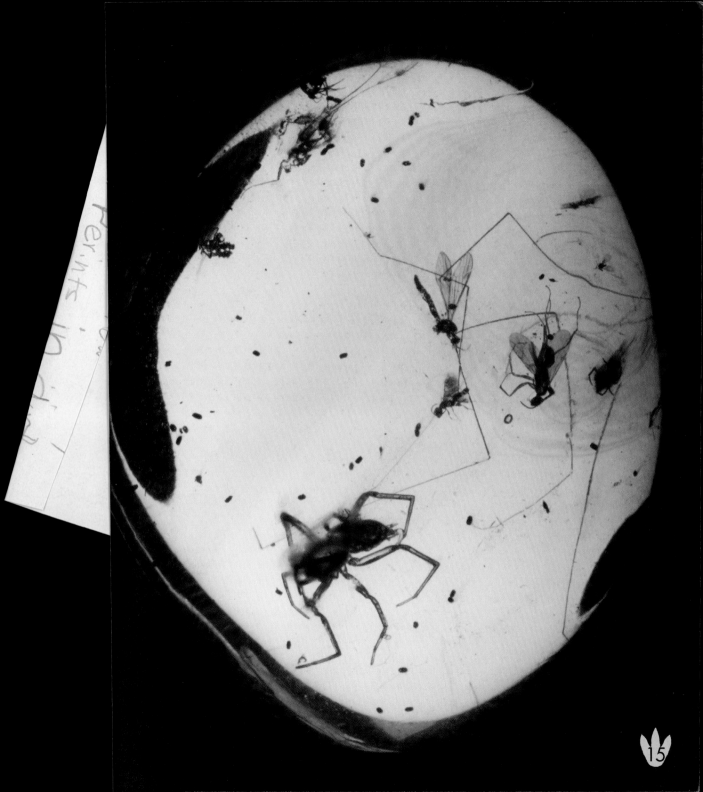

Finding fossils is fun. Fossils show us something about life long ago.

I can't wait to find more fossils. Can you?